Written by Christine Lazier
Illustrated by Paul Bontemps

Specialist adviser:
Celia Hawkesworth

ISBN 1 85103 100 6
First published 1990 in the United Kingdom
by Moonlight Publishing Ltd
36 Stratford Road, London W8
Translated by Sue Birchenall

© *1989 by Editions Gallimard*
English text © *1990 by Moonlight Publishing Ltd*
Typeset in Great Britain by Saxon Printing Ltd, Derby
Printed in Italy by La Editoriale Libraria

POCKET • WORLDS

The Horse

Horses and people haven't
always been companions...

The Ancient Greeks believed that lightning was carried across the skies by a great winged horse called Pegasus.

The unicorn of fairy-tales is a mythical horse with a single horn in the middle of its forehead.

The centaurs of Greek mythology were half man and half horse.

A prehistoric ancestor

Did you know that the horse's first ancestor, the Eohippus, was only as big as a fox? It lived sixty million years ago. Leaves were its main food, and it had four toes on each foot.

Very gradually, over millions of years, Eohippus grew larger. It became the size of a sheep, then as big as a pony. Soon it had only one toe which turned into a hoof. The teeth of these animals grew bigger and stronger, so they were able to munch grass.

The last of the horse's European ancestors, the Tarpan, was killed off by hunters. Its Asian cousin, Przewalski's horse, can still be seen in zoos, though probably none is left in the wild.

Przewalski's horses, named after the man who discovered them, are very difficult to train.

The first riders didn't have saddles or bridles; they steered the horses with their legs. This man is trying to lasso one of the wild horses that roamed in huge herds across the grassy steppes of Central Asia.

Prehistoric people hunted horses for their meat.

The terrified herds were sent galloping over the edge of a cliff, or driven into bogs and swamps where their legs sank into the soft ground so they couldn't escape.

Horses might have been killed off altogether if the nomads of Central Asia hadn't decided to tame the animals instead of killing them. In about 3,000 B.C., they began riding on horseback and training horses to pull their war-chariots.

The Scythian nomads were very skilful horsemen. Their warriors could fire showers of arrows as they galloped.

Early riders

It took a lot of skill and courage to gallop on a horse without a saddle or bridle. People soon realized that they could control the horse more easily by putting a bridle on its head, but it wasn't until about 400 B.C. that the Scythians invented the saddle, a leather frame padded with horsehair and held on by straps called girths. Stirrups, to rest your feet in as you rode, were probably invented by the Chinese in about the fifth century.

The Huns were fearsome Asian warriors who called themselves the Scourge of God.

The Mongols, led by Genghis Khan, conquered China before invading Europe. Mongol soldiers had five horses each, and officers sometimes had eighteen!

The nomads of Central Asia lived on horseback.

They fought, ate, even slept, mounted on their hardy little horses. They ate horsemeat and drank milk from the mares. The warriors were fierce, brutal men who destroyed everything in their path, and their horses were trained to travel long distances with little food. Attila, leader of the Huns, boasted, 'Where my horse has passed through, the grass will never grow again.'

Take a look at this horse.

Powerful muscles ripple beneath its shining coat. Its sharp eyes and sensitive nose are alert to any danger. Its ears prick towards the slightest sound. Each foot is protected by a horny covering, the hoof.

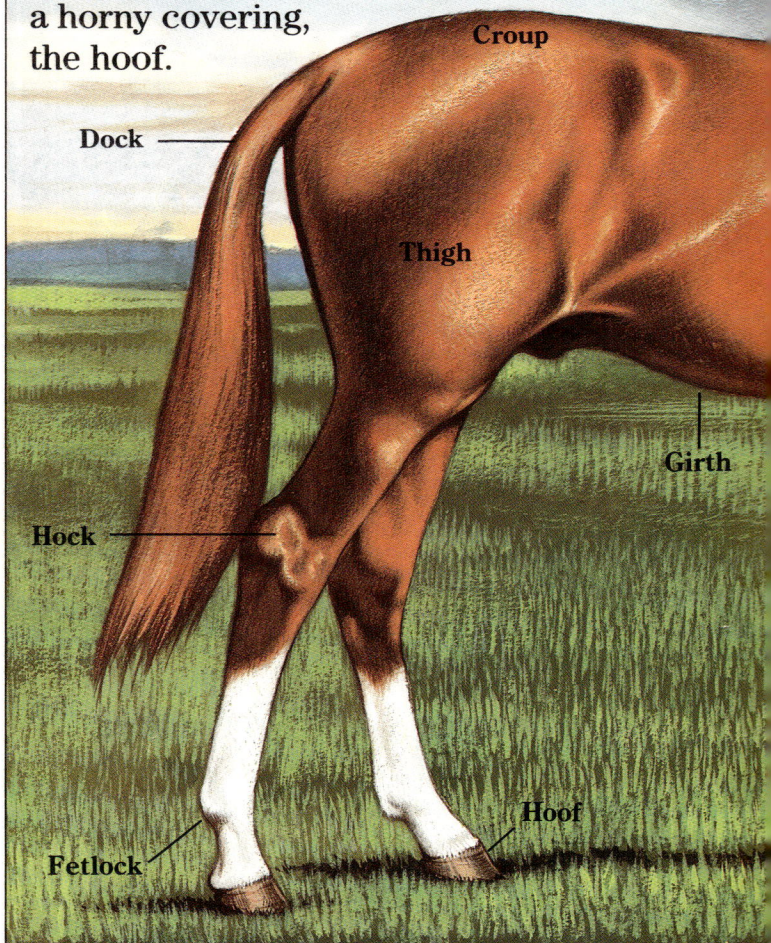

Croup

Dock

Thigh

Girth

Hock

Fetlock

Hoof

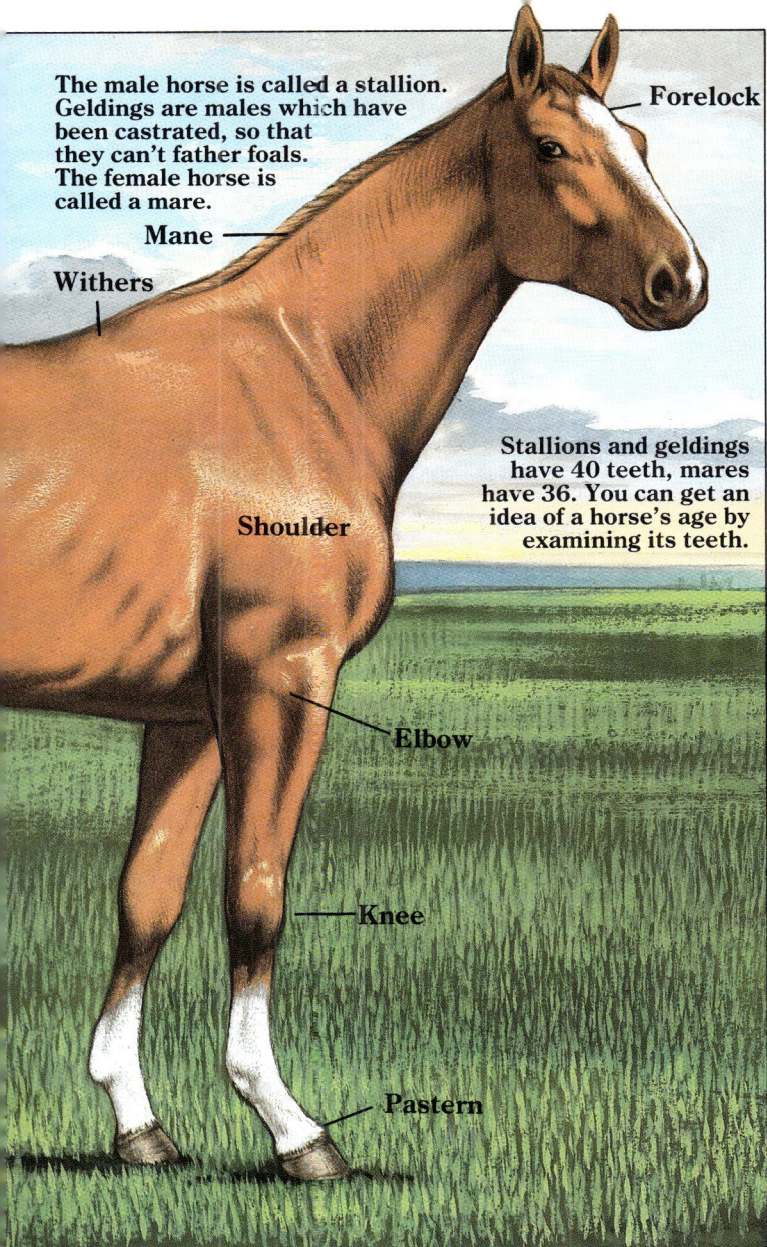

The male horse is called a stallion. Geldings are males which have been castrated, so that they can't father foals. The female horse is called a mare.

Forelock

Mane

Withers

Shoulder

Stallions and geldings have 40 teeth, mares have 36. You can get an idea of a horse's age by examining its teeth.

Elbow

Knee

Pastern

In the meadow, the horses doze in the
shade of the trees, swishing
their long tails to flick away flies.
One of them keeps watch.

Horses will lie down only if they feel absolutely safe.

Why do horses scratch themselves?
To get rid of insects or itchy mud
on their coats. When they are
wet, they roll in dust to dry themselves.

It's hard to reach all the itchy places!

Fences and trees make good scratching-posts.

Hay   **Oats**   **Barley**   **Alfalfa**

Horses spend more than half the day eating.

But unlike cows, horses aren't ruminants;
they have only one stomach. They eat
grass, hay, oats, bran, barley and carrots.
To tear off the grass, they twist it with
their top lip, wedge it between their teeth
and pull. Horses drink thirty litres of
water each day, and need to have blocks
of salt to lick. They are very greedy and
love bread and sugar.

This horse has
heard something.

And this horse looks
as if it's laughing!

This stallion has
scented a mare.

A herd of wild horses is led by the stallion, who fiercely defends his mares and their foals from the advances of other males. If two stallions meet face to face, they will fight. They rear up, lashing out with their hooves, and biting each other.

Before they fight, the stallions circle each other, snorting and pawing the ground with their hooves.

Herds of wild ponies still roam free across Dartmoor. Small and hardy and used to the harsh conditions on the moors, these ponies can be very stubborn, so they are not very good for riding. In the U.S.A., there are wild horses called mustangs. It takes a skilled cowboy to catch one and break it in.

Groups of semi-wild horses which live in the Camargue, in southern France ▶

Be careful – the mare will probably kick out at you if you go too near her foal.

This mare is gently licking her newborn foal.

Most foals are born in the spring.

After eleven months of pregnancy, the mare gives birth. The newborn foal has a lot of trouble balancing on its long, wobbly legs!

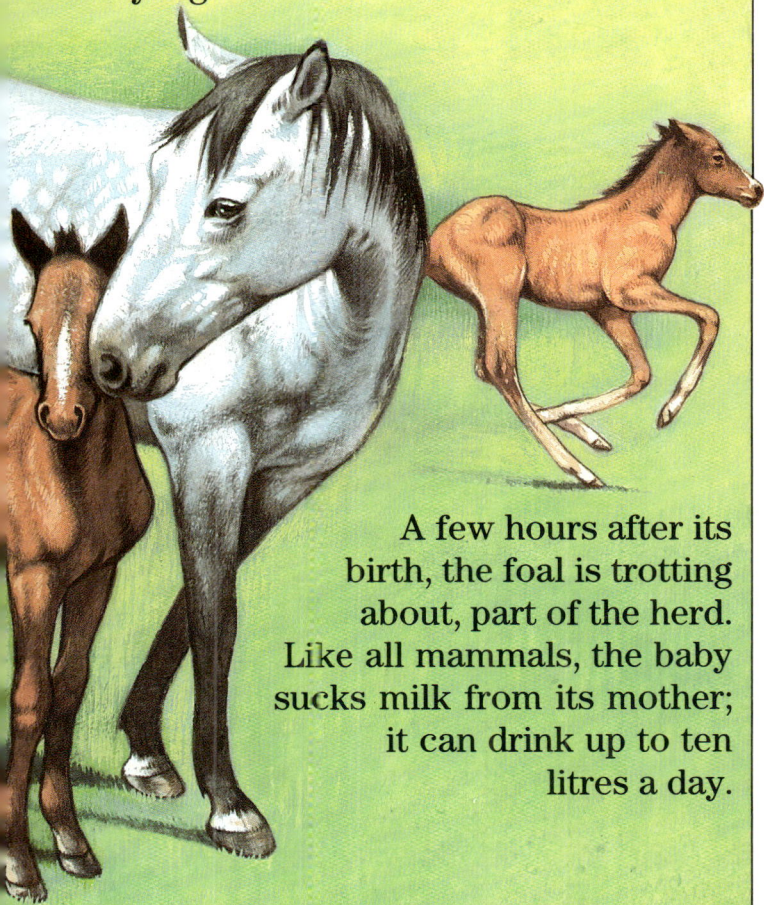

A few hours after its birth, the foal is trotting about, part of the herd. Like all mammals, the baby sucks milk from its mother; it can drink up to ten litres a day.

Foals are curious about everything, but they're very timid too. At the slightest sign of danger, they rush back to their mothers for protection.

In the days of the Ancient Greeks, this bronze statue was a gift to the gods at the shrine of Olympia, in Greece.

Training begins when the horse is about three years old.

By this time, it is strong enough to be ridden. But even before its first birthday, it can start learning to walk beside its trainer on a leading rein, and to obey simple commands. Then it has to get used to wearing a saddle and bridle.

When a horse walks, each hoof is placed on the ground in turn, one at a time.

This horse is trotting. Its hooves touch the ground in pairs, the left front leg with the right back leg, the right front with the left back.

Fastest of all is the gallop: the horse puts down first one back leg, then the other back leg with the opposite front one, and lastly the other front leg.

Before anyone tries climbing on its back, the horse is trained on a lunge, a long rein attached to the headcollar. This horse doesn't seem to like it much! Once the horse is obedient and responsive, it begins to learn more difficult exercises. Horses are often trained to jump, like the one in the illustration above.

The world's most famous horse-training school is the Spanish Riding School in Vienna. The amazing skill of their white Lipizzaner stallions thrills thousands of visitors every year.

Something is making this horse nervous.
The one on the right is neighing.

A horse kept in a stable should be groomed every day.

A rubber currycomb is used to scrub away mud before the horse's coat is brushed and its mane and tail combed.

1. Mane comb
2. Body-brush
3. Metal currycomb
4. Rubber currycomb

The hooves should be picked out to make sure that no stones are stuck under the shoes. It is important that the saddle and bridle fit well and are comfortable. When a horse has been taken out for a ride, it should be rubbed down with a handful of straw.

Why do horses need iron shoes?

To protect their hooves. First, the farrier heats up the shoe so that it can be shaped to the hoof. He trims the hoof, and then fixes on the shoe with eight nails. The red-hot shoe sizzles as he presses it on, but the horse doesn't feel a thing!

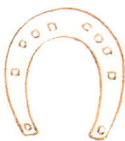

Horseshoe

Hoofpick

There are lots of different breeds of horse. You can see a few of them on this page.

Arab

Andalusian

Thoroughbred

Lipizzaner

Cob

Connemara

There are two main types of horse-race: a flat race, like the Derby, and a steeplechase, like the Grand National, where the horses have to jump over fences as they gallop round the circuit.

The thoroughbred is the fastest horse in the world.
All the best racehorses are thoroughbreds, born and raised on stud farms. Each foal is issued with special identity papers, and its name is entered into the General Stud Book. Every registered thoroughbred is descended from one of the three Arabian stallions brought to England three hundred years ago.

You don't always have to gallop to win a horse-race; in harness-racing, the horses are only allowed to trot. The driver rides in a small cart called a sulky.

Working horses

Around the Mediterranean, pack-horses still carry goods to market, usually in big baskets called panniers which hang beside the saddle.

Cart-horses did all the heavy work on the farm until machinery took their place. These two are pulling a plough.

Before cars were invented, people travelled in horse-drawn carriages.

Cart-horses are extremely strong.

Some can pull a load five times their own weight – quite a lot, because they sometimes weigh a thousand kilos! Once upon a time, the streets were full of horses towing all sorts of heavy loads.

This horse is pulling a cart laden with seaweed across a beach in Brittany, in northern France.

In recent times, some farmers have gone back to using horses instead of machinery, because they feel it is better for the land.

Horses used to help the farmer in lots of different ways; these are trampling corn to press out the grain.

In the Russian sport of kabachi, the rider tries to hurl a stick through a ring mounted on a long pole. This game is also played by South American cowboys, or gauchos, like the one on the right.

Sport on horseback

Polo was first played long ago in India and the East. Two teams of four riders try to hit a wooden ball with their mallets. The horses have to be fast, strong and very well-trained.

Gymkhanas are competitions for children and their ponies. There are lots of races and games, like riding in and out of a line of poles, or snatching up a tennis ball as they gallop.

Black-and-white ponies, like this mare and her foal,
are called piebalds.

This boy is about to put a rope halter over his pony's head.
Shetland ponies, like the one below, are small but strong.

Ponies are small horses, usually less than 1.50 m tall.

As long as they are treated kindly, they are friendly, gentle and reliable, though they can be very naughty if they think they can get away with it!

To make friends with your pony, you need to spend a few hours together every day, so that you get to know each other well. Try to move calmly and handle your pony confidently, because if you are nervous and jerky, it will make the pony nervous too.

Ponies are tough and strong. Some live to be more than forty years old.

The Falabella from Argentina is the smallest horse in the world. Falabellas are hardy, friendly and intelligent, and make lovely pets, but they are very expensive!

The horse's cousins

The zebra, with its black-and-white stripes, lives on the grassy plains of Africa. It's impossible to train a zebra. They bite and kick.

Small grey donkeys

Artists were painting the donkey in 6,000 B.C. Donkeys originally came from North Africa, so in cold, wet climates they need shelter during the winter. They are very sure-footed, and are often used to carry goods and people along perilous mountain paths. They are also extremely stubborn!

There are two types of Asiatic wild donkey: the Onager and the Kiang.

A hundred years ago, more than a hundred million wild donkeys roamed across Central Asia. Since then, most of them have been killed by hunters.

Coats of many colours

Horses' coats come in lots of different colours, each with a special name. Here are some of them.

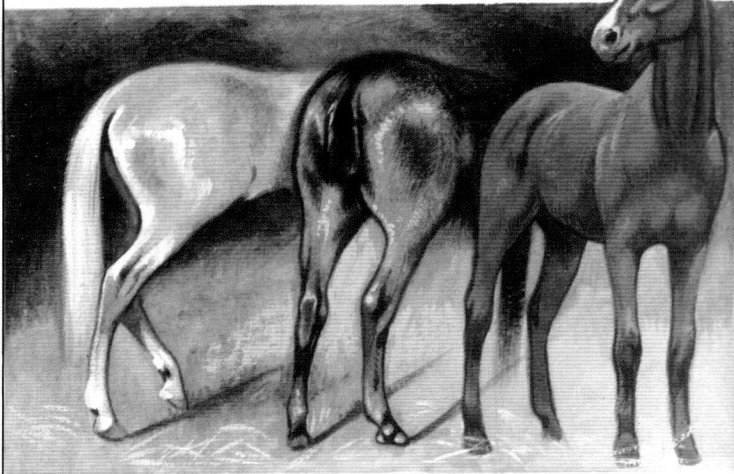

| Grey | Brown | Bay |

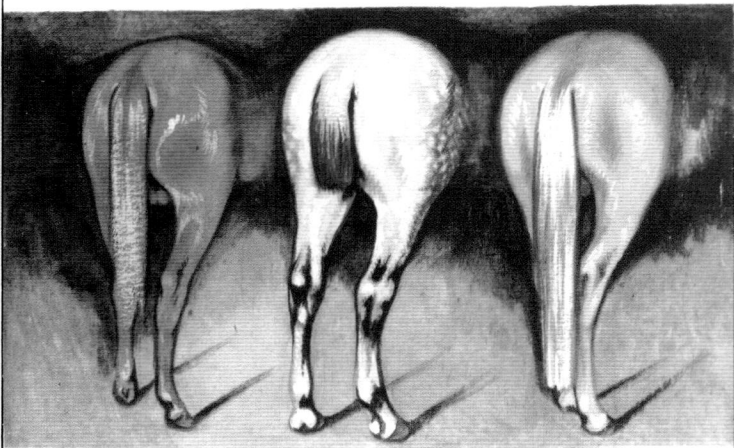

| Chestnut | Dapple grey | Palomino |

A white patch on a horse's forehead is called a 'star'. The bay pictured opposite has a 'blaze', a white streak down its face. White feet are called 'socks'.

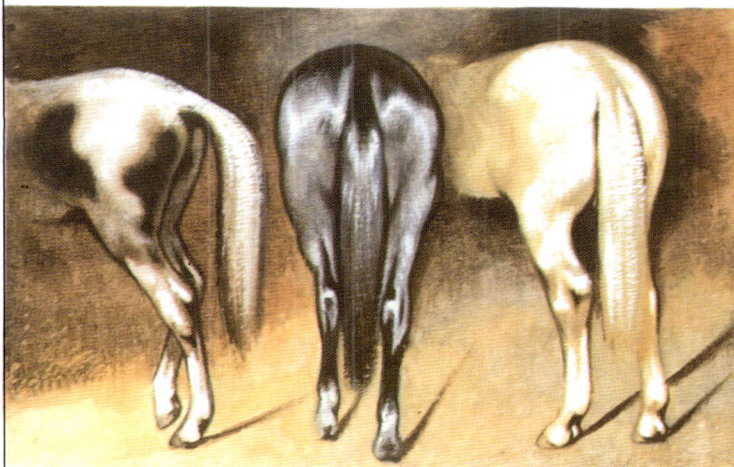

| Piebald | Black | Cream |

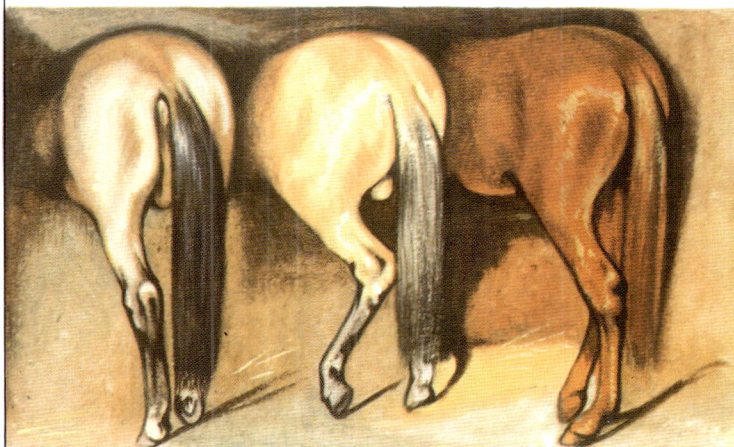

| Roan | Dun | Liver chestnut |

Index

**Pocket Worlds — building up into a
child's first encyclopaedia:**